FRANCIS FRITH'S

# HYTHE, ROMNEY MARSH AND ASHFORD PHOTOGRAPHIC MEMORIES

THE FRANCIS FRITH COLLECTION

www.francisfrith.com

Francis Frith's
# Hythe, Romney Marsh & Ashford

*Photographic Memories*

# Francis Frith's
# Hythe, Romney Marsh & Ashford

Paul Harris

First published in the United Kingdom in 2001 by
The Francis Frith Collection

Hardback edition 2001
ISBN 1-85937-360-7

Paperback edition 2001
ISBN 1-85937-256-2

Reprinted in hardback 2002

Reprinted in paperback 2006

British Library Cataloguing in Publication Data

Hythe, Romney Marsh & Ashford Photographic Memories
Paul Harris

The Francis Frith Collection
Frith's Barn, Teffont,
Salisbury, Wiltshire SP3 5QP
Tel: +44 (0) 1722 716 376
Email: info@francisfrith.co.uk
www.francisfrith.com

Printed and bound in Great Britain

*Front Cover:* Ashford, High Street 1901  47522t
*The colour-tinting is for illustrative purposes only, and is not intended to be historically accurate*

# Contents

# Francis Frith: *Victorian Pioneer*

**FRANCIS FRITH**, Victorian founder of the world-famous photographic archive, was a complex and multi-talented man. A devout Quaker and a highly successful Victorian businessman, he was both philosophic by nature and pioneering in outlook.

By 1855 Francis Frith had already established a wholesale grocery business in Liverpool, and sold it for the astonishing sum of £200,000, which is the equivalent today of over £15,000,000. Now a very rich man, he was able to indulge his passion for travel. As a child he had pored over travel books written by early explorers, and his fancy and imagination had been stirred by family holidays to the sublime mountain regions of Wales and Scotland. 'What a land of spirit-stirring and enriching scenes and places!' he had written. He was to return to these scenes of grandeur in later years to 'recapture the thousands of vivid and tender memories', but with a different purpose. Now in his thirties, and captivated by the new science of photography, Frith set out on a series of pioneering journeys to the Nile regions that occupied him from 1856 until 1860.

## Intrigue and Adventure

He took with him on his travels a specially-designed wicker carriage that acted as both dark-room and sleeping chamber. These far-flung journeys were packed with intrigue and adventure. In his life story, written when he was sixty-three, Frith tells of being held captive by bandits, and of fighting 'an awful midnight battle to the very point of surrender with a deadly pack of hungry, wild dogs'. Sporting flowing Arab costume, Frith arrived at Akaba by camel sixty years before Lawrence, where he encountered 'desert princes and rival sheikhs, blazing with jewel-hilted swords'.

During these extraordinary adventures he was assiduously exploring the desert regions bordering the Nile and patiently recording the antiquities and peoples with his camera. He was the first photographer to venture beyond the sixth cataract. Africa was still the mysterious 'Dark Continent', and Stanley and Livingstone's historic meeting was a decade into the future. The conditions for picture taking confound belief. He laboured for hours in his wicker dark-room in the sweltering heat of the desert, while the volatile chemicals fizzed dangerously in their trays. Often he was forced to work in remote tombs and caves where conditions were cooler. Back in London he exhibited his photographs and was 'rapturously cheered' by members of the Royal Society. His reputation as a photographer was made overnight. An eminent modern historian has likened their impact on the population of the time to that on our own generation of the first photographs taken on the surface of the moon.

## Venture of a Life-Time

Characteristically, Frith quickly spotted the opportunity to create a new business as a specialist publisher of photographs. He lived in an era of immense and sometimes violent change. For the poor in the early part of Victoria's reign work was a drudge and the hours long, and people had precious little free time to enjoy themselves. Most had no transport other than a cart or gig at their disposal, and had not travelled far beyond the boundaries of their own town or village. However,

by the 1870s, the railways had threaded their way across the country, and Bank Holidays and half-day Saturdays had been made obligatory by Act of Parliament. All of a sudden the ordinary working man and his family were able to enjoy days out and see a little more of the world.

With characteristic business acumen, Francis Frith foresaw that these new tourists would enjoy having souvenirs to commemorate their days out. In 1860 he married Mary Ann Rosling and set out with the intention of photographing every city, town and village in Britain. For the next thirty years he travelled the country by train and by pony and trap, producing fine photographs of seaside resorts and beauty spots that were keenly bought by millions of Victorians. These prints were painstakingly pasted into family albums and pored over during the dark nights of winter, rekindling precious memories of summer excursions.

## The Rise of Frith & Co

Frith's studio was soon supplying retail shops all over the country. To meet the demand he gathered about him a small team of photographers, and published the work of independent artist-photographers of the calibre of Roger Fenton and Francis Bedford. In order to gain some understanding of the scale of Frith's business one only has to look at the catalogue issued by Frith & Co in 1886: it runs to some 670 pages, listing not only many thousands of views of the British Isles but also many photographs of most European countries, and China, Japan, the USA and Canada – note the sample page shown on page 9 from the hand-written *Frith & Co* ledgers detailing pictures taken. By 1890 Frith had created the greatest specialist photographic publishing company in the

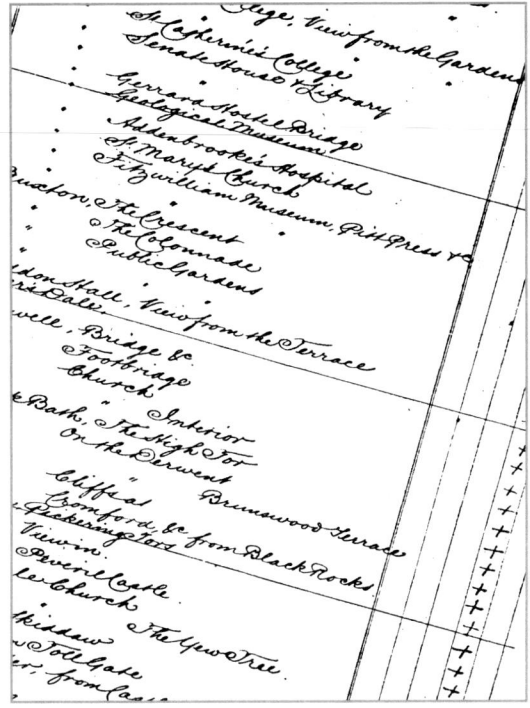

Frith's death, a new card measuring 5.5 x 3.5 inches became the standard format, but it was not until 1902 that the divided back came into being, with address and message on one face and a full-size illustration on the other. *Frith & Co* were in the vanguard of postcard development, and Frith's sons Eustace and Cyril continued their father's monumental task, expanding the number of views offered to the public and recording more and more places in Britain, as the coasts and countryside were opened up to mass travel.

Francis Frith died in 1898 at his villa in Cannes, his great project still growing. The archive he created continued in business for another seventy years. By 1970 it contained over a third of a million pictures of 7,000 cities, towns and villages. The massive photographic record Frith has left to us stands as a living monument to a special and very remarkable man.

world, with over 2,000 outlets – more than the combined number that Boots and W H Smith have today! The picture on the right shows the *Frith & Co* display board at Ingleton in the Yorkshire Dales (left of window). Beautifully constructed with a mahogany frame and gilt inserts, it could display up to a dozen local scenes.

### Postcard Bonanza

The ever-popular holiday postcard we know today took many years to develop. In 1870 the Post Office issued the first plain cards, with a pre-printed stamp on one face. In 1894 they allowed other publishers' cards to be sent through the mail with an attached adhesive halfpenny stamp. Demand grew rapidly, and in 1895 a new size of postcard was permitted called the court card, but there was little room for illustration. In 1899, a year after

# Frith's Archive: *A Unique Legacy*

**FRANCIS FRITH'S** legacy to us today is of immense significance and value, for the magnificent archive of evocative photographs he created provides a unique record of change in 7,000 cities, towns and villages throughout Britain over a century and more. Frith and his fellow studio photographers revisited locations many times down the years to update their views, compiling for us an enthralling and colourful pageant of British life and character.

We tend to think of Frith's sepia views of Britain as nostalgic, for most of us use them to conjure up memories of places in our own lives with which we have family associations. It often makes us forget that to Francis Frith they were records of daily life as it was actually being lived in the cities, towns and villages of his day. The Victorian age was one of great and often bewildering change for ordinary people, and though the pictures evoke an impression of slower times, life was as busy and hectic as it is today.

We are fortunate that Frith was a photographer of the people, dedicated to recording the minutiae of everyday life. For it is this sheer wealth of visual data, the painstaking chronicle of changes in dress, transport, street layouts, buildings, housing, engineering and landscape that captivates us so much today. His remarkable images offer us a powerful link with the past and with the lives of our ancestors.

## Today's Technology

Computers have now made it possible for Frith's many thousands of images to be accessed almost instantly. In the Frith archive today, each photograph is carefully 'digitised' then stored on a CD Rom. Frith archivists can locate a single photograph amongst thousands within seconds. Views can be catalogued and sorted under a variety of categories of place and content to the immediate benefit of researchers.

Inexpensive reference prints can be created for them at the touch of a mouse button, and a wide range of books and other printed materials assembled and published for a wider, more general readership - in the next twelve months over a hundred Frith local history titles will be published! The day-to-day workings of the archive are very different from how they were in Francis Frith's time: imagine the herculean task of sorting through eleven tons of glass negatives as Frith had to do to locate a particular sequence of pictures! Yet the

**See Frith at www. francisfrith.com**

archive still prides itself on maintaining the same high standards of excellence laid down by Francis Frith, including the painstaking cataloguing and indexing of every view.

It is curious to reflect on how the internet now allows researchers in America and elsewhere greater instant access to the archive than Frith himself ever enjoyed. Many thousands of individual views can be called up on screen within seconds on one of the Frith internet sites, enabling people living continents away to revisit the streets of their ancestral home town, or view places in Britain where they have enjoyed holidays. Many overseas researchers welcome the chance to view special theme selections, such as transport, sports, costume and ancient monuments.

We are certain that Francis Frith would have heartily approved of these modern developments in imaging techniques, for he himself was always working at the very limits of Victorian photographic technology.

## The Value of the Archive Today

Because of the benefits brought by the computer, Frith's images are increasingly studied by social historians, by researchers into genealogy and ancestory, by architects, town planners, and by teachers and schoolchildren involved in local history projects.

In addition, the archive offers every one of us an opportunity to examine the places where we and our families have lived and worked down the years. Highly successful in Frith's own era, the archive is now, a century and more on, entering a new phase of popularity.

## The Past in Tune with the Future

Historians consider the Francis Frith Collection to be of prime national importance. It is the only archive of its kind remaining in private ownership and has been valued at a million pounds. However, this figure is now rapidly increasing as digital technology enables more and more people around the world to enjoy its benefits.

Francis Frith's archive is now housed in an historic timber barn in the beautiful village of Teffont in Wiltshire. Its founder would not recognize the archive office as it is today. In place of the many thousands of dusty boxes containing glass plate negatives and an all-pervading odour of photographic chemicals, there are now ranks of computer screens. He would be amazed to watch his images travelling round the world at unimaginable speeds through network and internet lines.

The archive's future is both bright and exciting. Francis Frith, with his unshakeable belief in making photographs available to the greatest number of people, would undoubtedly approve of what is being done today with his lifetime's work. His photographs, depicting our shared past, are now bringing pleasure and enlightenment to millions around the world a century and more after his death.

# Hythe, Romney Marsh & Ashford
## *An Introduction*

THE PICTURESQUE LITTLE town of Hythe, the village-scattered, dyke-crossed expanse of Romney Marsh, and the modern expanding town of Ashford - these three are as different from each other as the proverbial chalk and cheese. An interesting and distinctive history, however, is common to them all, and fortunately much that has gone before has been recorded photographically.

Hythe was originally a port, one of the five known as the Cinque Ports, which would provide ships when King and country demanded. The other ports in the chain were Hastings, Romney, Dover and Sandwich.

Centuries before, the River Limen, now known as the Rother, entered the sea to the west of the present town at Portus Lemanis, or Port Lympne. Here, the Romans constructed one of their Saxon Shore forts in around the year AD 280. Recent historical opinion, however, disputes that this was constructed as a defence against Saxon raiders. It is more likely that the works were commissioned by the commander of the Classis Britannica (the British fleet), who seized power in Britain and declared the country independent of Rome. The commander, Carausius, was no doubt preparing for an onslaught by imperial troops sent to recover the province, a successful invasion that did occur ten years later.

By about 350 the fort had been abandoned; it gradually fell into ruins, which can still be seen

today. The reason for this abandonment may well have been linked to the silting up of Portus Lemanis - the Limen changed course to enter the sea at Romney. In fact, the twists and turns of the Limen have had a profound and continuing effect upon this part of Kent, as we shall see.

By the 8th century a Saxon settlement had been established a little further east at Sandtun. This later developed into a port where West Hythe now is. The silting-up process, combined with long-shore drift, eventually closed off this harbour too, leading in early medieval times to the birth of present-day Hythe. Around 1160, a striking new castle was built behind Hythe at Saltwood, reputedly on the foundations of an earlier Roman or Saxon structure. Saltwood Castle became infamous as the place where the assassins of Thomas Becket spent the night before committing their murderous act. In 1225 the fine church of St Leonard's was built. The crypt below has an assemblage of skulls and bones which have spawned much speculation as to their purpose and origin. By 1450 the retreating sea had left Hythe landlocked; its prosperity declined until 1575, when the granting of a charter provided a lifeline by allowing it to develop as a market town.

The threat from Napoleon brought a great deal of activity to this part of Kent, not least to Hythe. Part of the preparations against a possible French invasion involved the construction of numerous Martello Towers and of the Royal Military Canal, at huge and much-criticised public expense. Fortunately, they were not needed - Napoleon never invaded. The Canal, however, is much enjoyed today - ironically as a place of peace and refuge, a quiet scenic place in which to sit, walk or row a boat. The Royal Military Canal stretches for some 23 miles all the way around the old Saxon Shore to Winchelsea. In so doing, it half circumnavigates what the Reverend Richard Barham referred to as 'the Fifth Continent', Romney Marsh.

From the Light Railway Station in Hythe it has been possible since 1927 to travel across Romney Marsh all the way to Dungeness, stopping at the small Marsh towns and villages on the way, by courtesy of the world's smallest public railway. Superficially, the surrounding countryside may seem lacking in features and interest, but scratch beneath the surface and you will find that the area is rich in fascinating anecdotal history and tales of smugglers, ghosts and highwaymen. This has provided a never-ending source of inspiration for writers and artists through the years, many of whom have been drawn to the open skies and isolation of these remote places.

Dymchurch was once the capital of the Marsh. It was here that the notorious Lords of the Level sat; they meted out harsh justice, which was designed to ensure the survival of the remote Marsh communities against the ever-present danger of flooding from river and sea. Cutting down trees or even shrubs destined for use as part of the sea defence works could result in the severing of one's

ear - a penalty that is technically still in force today! It was in Dymchurch, specifically the Ship Inn, that the author Russell Thorndike penned the famous 'Dr Syn' stories of 19th-century smuggling.

Dymchurch, along with St Mary's Bay a little further along the coast, was also the home of the children's writer Edith Nesbit, best known for 'The Railway Children'.

New Romney, along with Dymchurch and Hythe, feature in H G Wells's tale 'Kipps'; the Reverend Richard Barham wrote 'The Ingoldsby Legends' when living in the thinly-populated marshes to the West; whilst in Old Romney churchyard stands the black monolithic grave of the late film producer Derek Jarman, who found endless inspiration amongst the shingle wastes of Dungeness.

The history of Romney Marsh is ancient indeed. Flint tools from the Bronze Age have been found near Lydd, Roman pottery has been discovered at Dymchurch, and evidence of Saxon settlement turned up at New Romney. Numerous ancient buildings dot the Marsh, including ruinous abandoned churches, picturesque ones still in use, old coaching inns, a 12th-century priory and the remains of early medieval sea walls long stranded by the changing contours of coastline and riverbank. In a dramatic example of the latter, the old medieval Rhee Wall now lies miles inland, alongside the A259. This came about after a devastating storm in 1287 which changed the course of the River Limen: ever afterwards it entered the sea at Rye, rather than at New Romney. The river is now known as the Rother, and it still occasionally bursts its banks during the winter. Never, though, has the river exceeded the depth of flooding it created in 1287; the tide marks of that flood are still visible on the pillars in St Nicholas's church at New Romney.

But just as at Hythe, it is more recent times that are addressed by the photographs presented in this book, the quiet rural and semi-rural life of our parents' and grandparents' generations. This life in itself was founded upon the firm bedrock of centuries of physical and social development. These fine pictures from the Frith archive give us a nostalgic glimpse into less hurried and perhaps more contented times.

To the north of Romney Marsh lies pleasant hilly countryside, a patchwork of fields and woodland dotted with many distinctive villages - some of them are represented by photographs in this book. In the heart of this rural area lies the town of Ashford. As a result of excavations connected to the Channel Tunnel project, it is now known that a Roman town once existed to the south-east of present-day Ashford; but the town we know today started much later, it would seem. First mentioned in the Domesday Book in 1086, the settlement soon developed into a market town, serving the farming communities of East Kent and Romney Marsh. Some fine medieval buildings still endure from these early days. Ashford really came into its own much more recently, though. By 1847, the

needs of the expanding railway network created a niche for Ashford as an important terminus for rail travel from miles around. Consequently the railway company decided to site its rolling stock workshops here.

Along with this development came extensive Victorian residential building to house the railway workers; this took the usual form of row upon row of terraced houses.

The pictures in this book cover the time from Ashford's railway industry heyday to the immediate post-war period. This is an important record for posterity, since the town has experienced much change since that time: the ring roads, extensive industrial estate and factory shop developments have appeared, and so has the Channel Tunnel, with its rail link, freight stop and International Railway Station. Now it seems that Ashford is to be the site for major residential development in its continuing role as an 'overspill' for Greater London, and as part of the Government's current plan to build many more new homes at selected sites in the south-east.

Already considerably altered in some places compared to twenty years ago, Ashford, Kent's boom town, is destined within a couple of decades to become virtually unrecognisable. Here, then, are some views of the Ashford that was; they were taken a century ago and also more recently, within the living memory of many local residents. Researching the history of Ashford along with Hythe and Romney Marsh has proven for me a fascinating experience. I hope the results of this endeavour, combined with the nostalgic images from the Frith archive, prove equally pleasurable for the reader.

# Hythe

**Hythe, General View 1890**  25731
This panoramic view of Hythe shows St Leonard's
Church in the foreground. The Royal Military Canal
stretches parallel with the coast, hidden by the
furthest trees in the middle distance. Note how
little the seafront is built up at this time.

**Hythe, The Church from the North-West 1890** 25733
Here we have an excellent view of the substantial church of St Leonard. Built in 1225, it occupies a commanding position over the town, as we have seen in view No 25731. The graveyard boasts a famous occupant, Lionel Lukin, the inventor of the lifeboat.

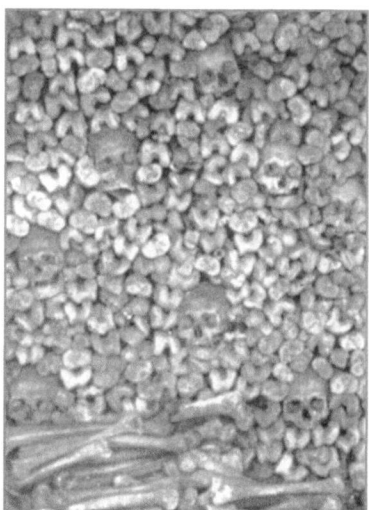

**Hythe, St Leonard's Church, The Charnel House 1903** 50381A
Beneath the church is an ambulatory, which contains a collection of human remains. Macabre though this seems, the practice was not uncommon during the Middle Ages, though few such collections exist today. The skulls and bones here pictured make up the remains of some 4,000 people, which are thought to have been disinterred from old graves to make way for new. Most of the remains seem to date from between the 12th and 15th centuries, though some may be up to 300 years older. What is particularly puzzling about the skulls is that they have marked Italian characteristics. It has been suggested that a pocket of Romano-Britons lived in the Hythe area for centuries after the departure of the Romans who had little to do with their Saxon neighbours. In time, their characteristics died out as the population mingled with newcomers during the Middle Ages.

**Hythe**
**High Street 1899** 44785
This view of the High Street before the advent of the motor
car shows an interesting building on the right. Here we have
J Coomber, Butcher, and the Rose and Crown Inn apparently
sharing the same property. This was a Mackeson public house -
Mackeson's brewed for many years in Hythe until 1968.

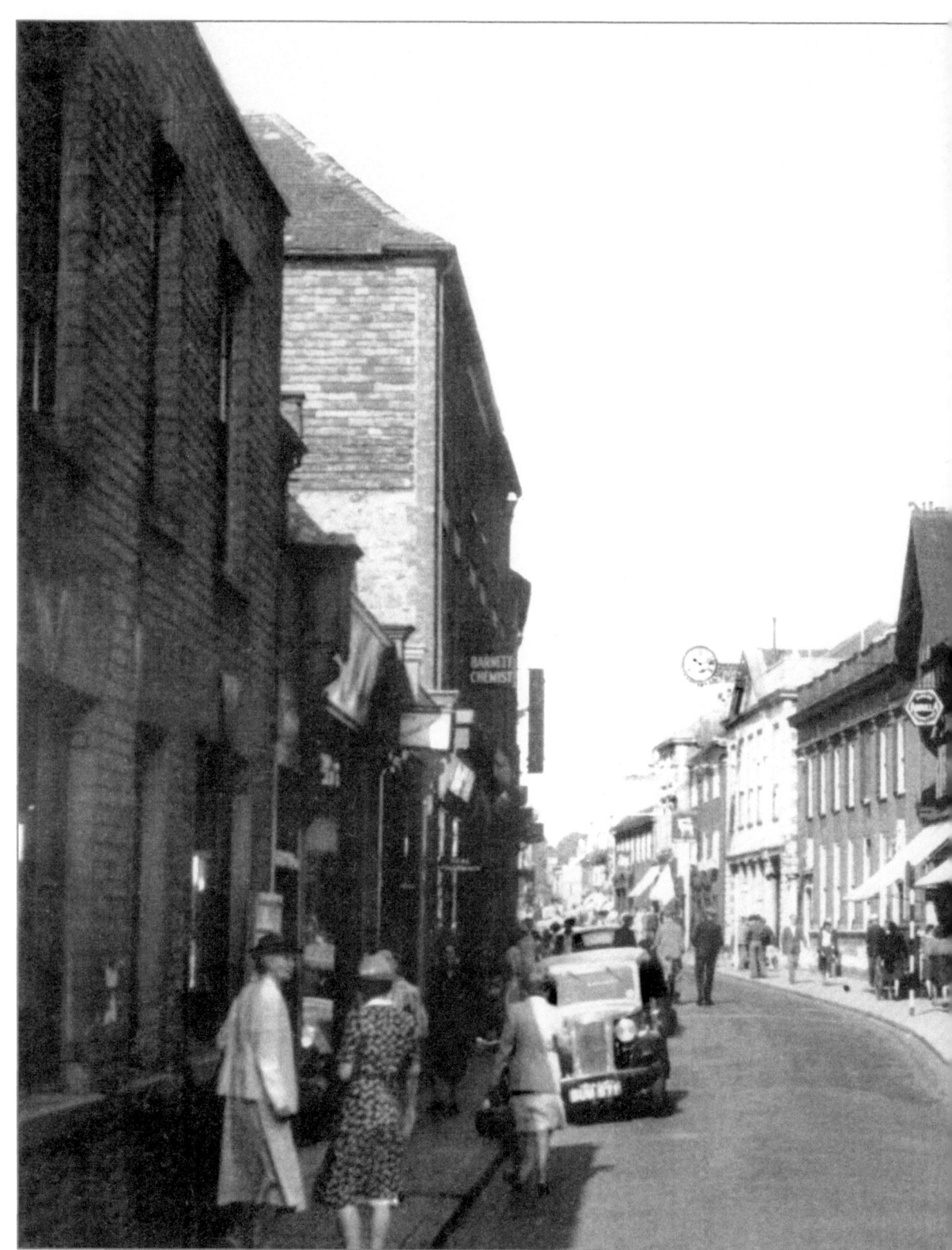

**Hythe, High Street c1945** H141010
It is a busy morning in the High Street on what seems to be a warm sunny day. It is interesting that the street is as devoid of cars then as it is now that it is pedestrianised.

▼ **Hythe, High Street, East c1955** H141019

This is a very quiet view of the east end of the High Street. Just beyond the 'Keep Left' signs today is a busy roundabout, though the High Street beyond is now semi-pedestrianised. The Oddfellows Hall is still there today.

▼ **Hythe, War Memorial 1921** 71097

Hythe's war memorial stands in The Grove, Prospect Road. A small winged angel, representing victory, holds a small model of a medieval Cinque Port vessel. The memorial commemorates 154 names from the First World War and 40 from the Second World War. In 1994 the bronze angel was stolen, but was replaced at considerable cost by Hythe Town Council.

▲ **Hythe, The Canal 1899**
44787
The Royal Military Canal was constructed in the early 19th century; its purpose was to transport military personnel along the most vulnerable stretch of Kent's coast in the event of a French invasion. The canal also served a second purpose as a defensive dyke, though it is hard to see it as much of an obstacle to an army that would have already crossed the Channel! This view, looking west, shows that boating was popular on the canal towards the end of the 19th century. H G Wells set a couple of scenes in his popular novel 'Kipps' on this canal.

**Hythe, The Canal
1918** 68153
We are looking east.
Note the soldier rowing
on the left. The First
World War would
have still been raging
in Europe when this
photo was taken; army
personnel were much
in evidence in the town,
either because they
were stationed at nearby
Shorncliffe Camp or
staying in a 'rest camp'
in Folkestone having
returned from action.

**Hythe, The Ladies' Walk 1918** 68151
This is a fascinating scene taken in pleasant surroundings. The 1918 fashions are interesting: they are a mixture of late Edwardian and what would become popular in the 1920s. Note the old perambulator being pushed by the child's mother, or nanny.

**Hythe, The Cricket Ground 1899** 44788 This quintessential English scene shows the Hythe Cricket Club at play. Who their opponents were on this occasion has long been forgotten, but it could have been a formidable foe, since the club was one of the most prestigious on the south coast. The club's earliest recorded match was in 1855.

◀ **Hythe, The Seabrook Hotel 1899** 44782
Built in 1880 on the site of the derelict Twiss Fort, the Seabrook Hotel was part of a much more ambitious plan to develop Hythe seafront which never saw the light of day. The hotel was renamed the Imperial in 1901, a name retained - along with the quality of the accommodation - to this day.

**Hythe, The Parade 1899** 44784
Note the changing tents on the beach, which were a feature of many seaside resorts in the Victorian and Edwardian period.

▼ **Hythe, The Parade 1899** 44783
Here we have a late Victorian beach scene. Note the light-coloured bathing carriages in the middle distance on the beach. We can also see a staggering nine Martello Towers stretching along the coast towards Romney Marsh. Many of these have now been demolished, or stand inaccessibly on the army firing range.

◄ **Hythe, Beaconsfield Terrace, Marine Parade 1903** 50375
We may be thankful that this fine, sturdy row of houses stands little changed today, outwardly at least. When this picture was taken, these were mostly complete houses; now, many are divided into flats. I wonder what the well-dressed Edwardian lady on the seat is reading?

**Hythe, The Parade
1918** 68149
It is 15 years after
photograph No 50375.
The fashions have
changed, a couple of
the buildings look a bit
shabby, and prams and
pushchairs are much in
evidence. Does anyone
recognise the little girl
who doesn't need to
ride in her pushchair
any more?

◀ **Hythe
The Promenade c1950**
H141035
It is a busy summer's day on Hythe seafront. The fashions have changed, and the Stade Court Hotel to the right of the picture displays a more modern architectural style. In the distance you can see that the number of Martello Towers has considerably decreased.

### Hythe, The Beach 1918
68150
This picture was taken a little further west than No 68149, and probably on the same day. Note that we now have stationary changing huts, rather than bathing machines - they look a bit like today's portaloos! There is an interesting collection of people lounging about here, and quite a variety of different hats!

### Hythe
### The Promenade c1950
H141049
Here we see the motorcar coming into its own. On the left, in the middle distance, the squat white building is the Four Winds Café. The sea wall appears to have been much strengthened and improved since the earlier pictures.

### Hythe, The Ponies c1960  H141077
Here we see that staple ingredient of the early post-war seaside holiday, the donkey ride - or rather, in this case, the pony ride. Beyond the ponies, note the pre-BT telephone box, which already looks dated, and a good view of the wooded hills behind the town.

▼ **Saltwood, The Village Hall and the Almshouses 1902** 48832

Saltwood dates back to at least the year 833, when it is mentioned as a land grant by King Egbert. Archaeological discoveries over the last couple of years may push the date of the area's habitation back further. During the building of the Channel Tunnel Rail Link, numerous graves of Saxon warriors were found; some of the warriors still clasped swords in their hands. From medieval times onwards, almshouses were established to house poor families. Those built for the poor of Saltwood can be seen stretching back from the unusual and attractive village hall. This view is from the village green.

▼ **Saltwood, The Castle 1890** 25896

This was formerly the home of the late Alan Clark MP, author of the famous 'Diaries'. Saltwood Castle as we see it today is a largely 13th-century castle, thanks to the additions and improvements made then. However, it is believed that earlier forts were established here during Roman and Saxon times. The knights who murdered Thomas Becket spent the night here before riding to Canterbury.

▲ **Saltwood, The Castle 1902** 48830
This idyllic view of Saltwood Castle makes us realise just how unspoiled many rural areas were only a century ago. Nowadays, the castle does not present such a dramatic aspect from here, owing to more mature tree growth.

**Hythe, Slaybrook 1903** 50382
Slaybrook is the name of a little babbling brook that runs beneath the road between Saltwood and Sandling. We may be thankful that this beautiful 16th-century house, Slaybrook Hall, has been well preserved and even enhanced. Today the building is somewhat more extensive than we see here, but the additions are in completely the original style; you would never know that they are modern from the outside. The site is more open now - the trees have been felled. Slaybrook Hall is reputedly haunted by a number of ghosts, according to ghost hunter Peter Underwood, who gives details in his book 'Ghosts of Kent'.

**Hythe**
**The Station 1928** 80396
Here is the world's smallest public railway in action. The Romney,
Hythe and Dymchurch Railway was the brainchild of Henry
Greenly, Captain J E P Howey and Louis Zborowski. The railway
opened for business in 1927. Tragically, Zborowski was killed in a
road accident before he could see his dream realised.

# Romney Marsh

**Dymchurch**
**The Main Road 1927**  80403
The main road through Dymchurch looks remarkably empty.
The garage just visible in the foreground to the right was the first
to have a petrol pump in Dymchurch. Where the two ladies are
walking on the other side of the road in front of the set-back
building is now the bus stop and public toilets.

**Dymchurch
The Sands 1927** 80400
The beach here has
always been popular,
though it is a lot sandier
now than when this
picture was taken. Note
the bathing tents lined
up along the top of
the beach. We may be
thankful that today the
ugly telegraph poles
have all gone. Martello
Towers can be seen
landward of the bathing
tents.

### ◄ Dymchurch
### High Street 1921
71107
We are looking the other way from view No 80403. One of the line of cottages in the foreground was once home to Edith Nesbit, the children's author, famous for 'The Railway Children' and 'The Treasure Seekers'. Nesbit was well-known around Dymchurch for her bohemian ways and arty friends.

### ◄ St Mary's Bay, The Stores c1960
S538032
Here we have a former wartime building used as a general stores during the heyday of St Mary's Bay as a holiday destination for children. The golden beaches that made this possible are still as beautiful, but the holiday camp has gone and so has this shop. This site is now overgrown waste ground, and St Mary's Bay is primarily made up of modern housing development. Just down the road from here stand two Nissen huts, the final home of Edith Nesbit. Appropriately for the author of 'The Railway Children', these stand next to the line of the Romney, Hythe and Dymchurch railway.

▼ **New Romney, North Street c1955** N141007
This beautiful street is typical of the parts of New Romney that are away from the main through road. Even today North Street is quiet like this, although there are more parked cars, of course. On the left-hand side of the road, just before the telegraph pole, is an establishment called 'Gables', apparently a carvery and bar. This is now the Broadacre Hotel.

▼ **Lydd, The Rype c1955** L333007
The Rype is the name of the green we see here. We are looking towards the centre of this small town, which is dominated by its impressive 13th-century church. Lydd is somewhat empty and windswept, and this picture gives the impression this was always so; but to many who live on the Marsh, it is this lonely isolation that is so appealing.

▲ **Lydd, Ferryfield Airport c1955** L333030
The fortunes of this remote little airport have fluctuated widely over the years. Here we see the novel sight of cars being loaded onto aircraft for flights across the Channel. The operator at this time, Silver City Airways, carried on for many years right up until the late 1970s.

**Dungeness, The Romney, Hythe and Dymchurch Railway c1960** D165010
Little has obviously changed here over the years since this picture was taken. The railway still runs, and uses very similar engines and rolling stock. The little station has expanded slightly, and the area now boasts a well-laid-out bird reserve. Out of sight, though, are two large nuclear power stations, which were built between 1960 and 1984.

**◄ Bilsington, The Canal Bridge 1909** 61580A
The Royal Military Canal on its way from Hythe runs beneath the hills upon which Bilsington stands. There is today a public footpath the length of the canal all the way to Rye.

### ◄ Bilsington
### The Village 1909
61578

Four miles inland and overlooking Romney Marsh from the old cliffs of the Saxon Shore, Bilsington displays architecture typical of this part of Kent, notably the white weatherboarding seen here. The building in the middle of this picture seems to be a wagon maker's yard.

### ▼ Bilsington, The Priory 1909
61579

This attractive old priory was founded in 1253 for an order of Augustinian monks. There are frequent reports of ghostly monks walking and chanting in the vicinity, including a sighting by the wife of the writer Joseph Conrad. The strange needle-like obelisk that stands outside the village is in memory of a former owner of this priory, who fell from a stage coach in 1835.

### ◄ Ruckinge, The Village
### 1909 61572

Cars now race through here - it is hard to imagine that it once was as empty and quiet as this! The house on the right is the Post Office. Somehow we cannot imagine there ever being a queue here.

**Orlestone, The Church c1960** 0136012
This ancient parish is now part of Ham Street. The church, although it is very old, has a Victorian interior; but it has an attractive and distinctive appearance, as we can see.

**Ham Street, The Village 1909** 61575
This is the main street through the village, which is apparently absolutely deserted - the photograph was taken in much quieter times. Since the period of the picture, there has been a lot of modern housing development here.

**Ham Street**
**The High Street c1965**  H505014
By the 1960s, the village has gained road markings
and telephone poles. The tobacconist's shop,
F Tippen and Son Ltd, is stocking the ubiquitous
'Woodbine' cigarettes.

**Ham Street, The Cross Roads c1965** H505041
Here we have a good view of the attractive house on the cross roads of the Tenterden, Ashford and Romney Marsh roads. The 'Keep Left' signs look the same as today's, and the clothes and hairstyles of pedestrians don't look out of place either. Today, though, there is usually a constant stream of motor traffic here.

**Smallhythe, The Village 1900** 45007
This is a fascinating little village with some interesting buildings. Here we can see the red brick church of Flemish design, and beyond it the attractive black and white timbered Priests House. Further down the lane we can see another house, also timbered - it was built in 1480. This was once the home of the harbour master, which shows just how far the sea used to come in during the Middle Ages. The actress Ellen Terry lived in the house from 1919 until her death. The house is now in the care of the National Trust, and open to the public.

# Ashford

**Ashford, The View from the Church 1901** 47520
Ashford is a bustling modern town that developed with the
railway, but it was mentioned in the Domesday Book of 1086.
This old-established market town is dominated by the great
pinnacled tower of its 15th-century church, which is pleasantly
situated in a square. Today, offices jostle near to the railway,
Ashford International Station and the motorway.

**Ashford**
**High Street 1901** 47522
This quiet empty street pictured here contrasts with the bustle
of today's pedestrianised area, which is often occupied by
a busy market. Centre left of the picture we can see a Bon
Marché shop; the Bingo Hall now stands on this site.

**Ashford, High Street
1906** 53444
This is a lovely view a
little further west along
the High Street during
the heyday of horse-
drawn vehicles. Just
behind the ornamental
fountain can be seen an
oblong light-coloured
object attached to
the wall of the
building behind. This
is the town's official
thermometer; I wonder
what it reads on this
obviously sunny
morning?

**Ashford, High Street c1950** A71007

Looking east along the High Street, we can see on the left that the Co-operative Society shop is not yet in the building with the public clock; the Central Stores occupy it at this date. Two doors down the road is the Westminster Bank, still the National Westminster today. In the distance, the High Street can be seen to continue further than today - the busy ring road now cuts through this area.

**Ashford, High Street 1901** 47521

Although the street layout at this point is the same today, most of the buildings have changed beyond recognition. On the left, note the interesting top hat trade sign above a shop awning. A little further down the street, a boy carries a billboard advertising 'Hilton's Boot Sale'. Note the building in the centre by the attractive street lamp - we will see it again.

**Ashford**
**High Street c1950** A71010
This is a very similar view to No 47521 (opposite page, below),
but taken half a century later. Not only are there (predictably now)
plenty of cars to be seen, but many more people as well. Note the
classical-looking building at the centre of the picture, which has
completely changed from the earlier view. This building is not as
old as it looks: it is a 20th-century creation, built in 1927.

▲ **Ashford, High Street**
◀ **1901** 47523
This lovely detailed
view shows the west
end of the High Street.
The Castle Commercial
Hotel later became the
Castle pub, which has
since closed. Pilchers,
the boot and legging
makers, has since
become the premises
of Woolworths.

**Ashford, Bank Street 1903** 50331
We are looking up Bank Street towards the town. Four doors up on the right is accommodation for cyclists. Cycling was a popular hobby then as now. Note the interesting group of children on the left: the little boy standing in the road is leaning on a hoop. The shops here have all gone, and have been replaced by others.

**Ashford**
**North Street c1950** A71019
Here we have a typical 1950s street scene in what was the main route
out from Ashford to Canterbury. During the 1980s, North Street was
pedestrianised; it terminated at the ring road which surrounds the town
centre, which creates in effect a large traffic island.

**Ashford, The Parish Church c1960** A71079
Said to be one of the finest town churches in Kent, the parish church is built of Kentish ragstone and has an impressive interior. The tower stands 121ft high, and the church can seat up to 1,700 people. A famous curate was the Reverend Richard Barham, who later moved to Romney Marsh and wrote the 'Ingoldsby Legends'.

**Ashford, Church Road 1901** 47525
This scene is recognisable today only by the presence of the parish church in the distance. Both the Congregational Church and the houses next to it on the left were demolished in the 1970s to make way for the town's Magistrates Court.

**Ashford, Lower High Street c1960** A71064
Here we have another view of the High Street before pedestrianisation. It is interesting that some things have not changed: the Co-operative Society shop is still in the same building, for instance, on the right with the clock above the shop sign. Next door is a Pricerite supermarket. In later years the town's Job Centre occupied these premises; today it is the site of the Careers Office.

**Ashford, Church Square c1960** A71075
This remains a quiet oasis in an otherwise bustling town. Here office workers can eat their lunchtime sandwiches in peace. The old building second door up on the left was once the town's Grammar School, founded by Norton Knatchbull in 1635. It now houses the town museum, which is open from April to October. Next to this now stands the Tourist Information Centre.

### ◄ Ashford, High Street and the Church 1901  47524

Here we see the Parish Church as we look from the High Street through Middle Row, part of the 'old town' of Ashford. On the left can be seen the drinking fountain, which was built over a natural spring; it operated until 1930. There is now an ornamental fountain a little further east along the High Street. Note the oyster and ice merchant behind the fountain, where estate agents Mann and Co now are. On the right we can also see the town thermometer attached to a wall, as an earlier view showed.

### ▼ Ashford, The Roman Catholic Church c1908  60333

There is an interesting group in front of the attractive church. The man in the white hat in the background and the three boys in front of him are all looking this way. Are they watching the girl pushing the pram, or the photographer? The church itself was built in 1865, but congregations dwindled over the years; the building was replaced in 1990.

### ◄ Ashford The Grammar School 1901  47531

This is a fine clear photograph of this ivy-clad school building with its typical Victorian architecture and interesting bell tower. The school was built in the 1880s, and is now the Ashford North School.

**Ashford, The War Memorial c1955** A71037
The second of the two major wars, the dead of which are commemorated in this memorial, would have still been fresh in the memories of the people sitting here. This scene remains unchanged today.

**Ashford, The Hare and Hounds Public House at Potters Corner 2004** A71704
During the 13th and 14th centuries a large amount of pottery was produced in the vicinity of Potters Corner; the amount of waste that has been discovered here indicates that the production was on an industrial scale. The Hare and Hounds public house now stands at Potters Corner. Note the toll collector's cottage at the entrance to Sandyhurst Lane in this photograph.

**Ashford, Victoria Park, the Hubert Fountain 1921** 70312
One lasting legacy to the people of Ashford from the late Victorian era of public works for the social well-being of the townsfolk is Victoria Park, the largest open recreational space within the town. The land for this was bought in 1898, in order to create a public park from land previously leased as playing fields. The Hubert Fountain, which now dominates much of the park, was formerly in the grounds of Olantigh, Wye. It had first appeared as an exhibit in the Second International Exhibition of 1862 in the Royal Horticultural Society gardens, London. The fountain has been restored in recent years and now works again after many years of neglect. The stags have been removed, however.

**Ashford, The Cottage Hospital 1908** 60335
Built in 1878, the Cottage Hospital was financed initially by a local banker, Mr W P Pomfret, as a memorial to his late wife. Maintenance of the hospital was remarkably almost entirely due to voluntary contributions from the people of Ashford. The hospital was auctioned in 1928.

▼ **Ashford, East Hill, Old Cottages 1903** 50333

These 16th-century cottages were much beloved by artists and photographers over the years. However, they did cause a severe traffic congestion problem during the 1920s and 1930s as vehicles swerved outwards to avoid the protruding buildings and thus blocked the oncoming traffic. This problem was especially acute as East Hill was the main road to and from Folkestone and Dover at the time. Eventually the buildings were demolished to make way for a car park! The large wooden panelled gates further up the road on the left were an entrance to part of the property of Ashford School, which occupied both sides of the road.

▼ **Ashford, Canterbury Road c1908** 60331

Two well-dressed Edwardian ladies push cycles past the large houses of the wealthy along Canterbury Road. Note the attractive street lamp behind them on the right. The scene is delightfully rural compared to today.

▲ **Ashford, Magazine Road c1908** 60329

These attractive houses show interesting mock-Tudor features. Other points of interest are the ornamental street lamps, and the curious scatter of people in the road. They look as if they have all been orchestrated into appropriate poses; have we perhaps seen them in other pictures in the series? The name Magazine Road comes from the one-time army ammunition and provisions store at the end of this road.

◄ **Ashford**
**Western Avenue c1908**
60328
The fine sweep of this road with its large Victorian semi-detached houses shows late 19th-century residential architecture at its best. The road seems curiously grimy, though, probably as a result of mud and manure deposited by horse-drawn vehicles.

**Ashford, Godinton Road c1908** 60327
Where now heavy traffic pours both ways along this road, children played in the street early this century. The only vehicles in evidence are a cart pushed by two boys, and in the distance a bicycle being ridden.

**Ashford
The Livestock Market
1906** 53445
Here we see the arrival of droves of Romney Marsh sheep. Farmers were criticised at the time for driving the sheep on foot too long a distance, from the Marsh all the way to Ashford. The fine-looking stagecoach belongs to the Saracens Head Hotel. A coach sometimes accompanied these movements of livestock, in case any became too tired to go on and needed a lift! It seems extremely unlikely, though, that a smart hotel coach would have been used for this purpose. The large pillared building is the premises of agricultural and mechanical engineers Frederick Clark.

**Ashford from the Air 1961** AFA95322

◀ **Godinton House 1901**  47562
Godinton House, built in the
17th century, was home to many
generations of Tokes. The last owner
left the house to a charitable trust so
that it would be looked after for years
to come. The most well-known Toke
was Captain Nicholas Toke, who gave
the house its unique decorations.
In the wooden panelling there are
carved figures carrying out pike and
musket drill - many of the drills are
continued today by the Honourable
Artillery Company. Captain Toke led
a full active life, outliving five wives.
He was apparently making his way to
London to find his sixth wife when he
died. He was only 93!

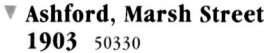

### Ashford, Elwick Road
**1901** 47526

This photograph was taken a century ago, and a world away from the same road today, which seems at times like a public motor-racing circuit - it is now part of the Ashford ring road. Again we see attentive pedestrians, and manure going to waste in the road!

### Ashford, Marsh Street
**1903** 50330

This street is now known as Station Road, and is part of the ring road. Almost every building we can see here has since been demolished. The one notable exception is the imposing Baptist Church building on the left-hand side of the road. Opposite to this can be seen a bicycle wheel trader's sign above Randalls, the bicycle and tricycle manufacturer; a large office block now occupies the site.

### Ashford, Station Road
**c1950** A71002

Were it not for the public house on the right, this scene would be completely unrecognisable. The Kent Arms is now the Fat Fiddler public house. Up the road on the right beyond the pub now stand Crouch's garage, the Royal Mail Sorting Office, Kent House and the Ashford bowling alley. Note the traffic policeman standing in the road - he is hardly needed, we might think.

# Around Ashford

**Ashford, Willesborough Windmill c1960** A71080
This windmill, which today stands beside the busy
M20 motorway, was built in 1869. At the time
this picture was taken, the mill would have had an
electric motor to make sure it still operated in calm
weather. Willesborough was not incorporated into
Ashford Urban District until 1934.

**Kennington, The Mill 1901** 47543
Like Willesborough, Kennington had a working mill. This one, though, was a combined wind, steam and watermill. The windmill was built in 1813, and the steam and water elements were added later.

### Kennington
### The Village 1901

47540

A tranquil scene, which shows another village that has since become absorbed by Ashford's burgeoning residential development. Some of these houses display the exterior weatherboarding much used in this part of Kent.

### Kennington
### The Church 1901

47541

This is an attractive limestone church with some medieval features that have been restored. The interior is Victorian, but the tower is 15th-century. Note the St George's flag, which seems to be at half mast.

### Hothfield, The Church 1901  47549

This attractive late medieval church was partially restored inside by Sir John Tufton after a fire, which had caused considerable damage. There is a monument to Sir John, his wife and family: alabaster effigies lie on a marble table tomb.

▼ **Hothfield, Hothfield House 1901** 47544

This imposing house is set in gardens in countryside; amidst much beautiful parkland. The pointed steeple of Hothfield church can just be seen in the distance on the right.

▼ **Great Chart, The Village 1908** 60339

Great Chart is a very attractive village just outside Ashford, with some charming traditional cottages. The children playing in the street look very photogenic; the one sitting down seems to be wearing a very unusual hat.

▲ **Great Chart
The Village 1908** 60337

One of the houses here seems completely covered in ivy, a feature noticeable on a number of old photographs. This is one of those pictures where the people look deliberately posed, especially the ones standing at intervals down the left-hand side of the road.

◀ **Great Chart**
**The Village 1901** 47551
Note the almshouse just
beyond the horse and cart
on the right. On the left we
see another fine example of
a windmill.

**Woodchurch, All Saints' Church c1955** W408004 ▷
This is a well-restored 13th-century church; some locally-mined Bethersden marble was used in its construction. The village of Woodchurch itself is large. A wide expanse of green is surrounded by weatherboarded cottages and Tudor houses.

**Pluckley, The Village 1901** 47566 ▽
Pluckley today has become synonymous with ghosts. In all, there were said to be twelve or thirteen active ghosts here, according to author and ghost hunter Andrew Green. On a recent visit, however, Green found that only one haunting seemed to be still active. This related to the Black Horse public house pictured here. Apparently, a barmaid walking home past the adjacent graveyard in 1996 saw a woman dressed in red moving about among the gravestones as if looking for one in particular. The barmaid only realised that there was something strange going on when the woman in red passed through two of the gravestones!

**Pluckley**
**The Village Square c1950**  P57001
We are beside the Black Horse, with the church beyond. Note the
windows with curved-topped frames. This design of window can be
found all over Pluckley: they are known as 'Dering' windows,
after the local family that popularised them.

**Brook, The Post Office c1955** B583007
This rather long straggling village is appropriately named, as a little brook does indeed run through the village beside the road. Set in attractive countryside beside the North Downs, Brook is today a dormitory village for Ashford to some extent. Little has changed here over the years.

**Brabourne Lees**
**The Village c1955** B578005
A small village beneath the North Downs,
Brabourne Lees has changed little. Note
the garage on the left with the old petrol
pumps and Castrol signs.

**Bethersden, Forge Corner c1955** B571005
The village of Bethersden is famous for the marble once quarried there. Examples of Bethersden marble can be found in the cathedrals of Canterbury and Rochester, as well as in many local churches. The white weatherboarding typical of villages in the Weald of Kent is well represented here.

**Bethersden, Forge Hill c1955** B571004
The good road surface seen here contrasts with the situation in the 18th century. Then, the well-to-do of the area used to have their coaches drawn by oxen in order to negotiate safely the boggy roads, which in bad weather were reputed to be the worst in Kent.

**Ashford, Eastwell Park c1865**  7080
Although this site has been occupied and built upon at least since medieval times, it is surprising that the current imposing building was built as recently as 1928, a replica Elizabethan mansion. The building seen here in this early photograph was constructed around 1790. By 1900, the mansion had been enlarged and another tower added.

**Eastwell, The Church and the Lake 1901**  47539
The church and the house amongst the trees beside the lake in Eastwell Park make a haunting and atmospheric view. In these grounds stands the Bethersden marble tomb of Richard Plantagenet, son of Richard III. It had been much vandalised over the years, but it has recently been restored by local author Michael Jack.

# Index

# FRITH PRODUCTS & SERVICES

Francis Frith would doubtless be pleased to know that the pioneering publishing venture he started in 1860 still continues today. Over a hundred and forty years later, The Francis Frith Collection continues in the same innovative tradition and is now one of the foremost publishers of vintage photographs in the world. Some of the current activities include:

## INTERIOR DECORATION

Today Frith's photographs can be seen framed and as giant wall murals in thousands of pubs, restaurants, hotels, banks, retail stores and other public buildings throughout the country. In every case they enhance the unique local atmosphere of the places they depict and provide reminders of gentler days in an increasingly busy and frenetic world.

## PRODUCT PROMOTIONS

Frith products are used by many major companies to promote the sales of their own products or to reinforce their own history and heritage. Frith promotions have been used by Hovis bread, Courage beers, Scots Porage Oats, Colman's mustard, Cadbury's foods, Mellow Birds coffee, Dunhill pipe tobacco, Guinness, and Bulmer's Cider.

## GENEALOGY AND FAMILY HISTORY

As the interest in family history and roots grows world-wide, more and more people are turning to Frith's photographs of Great Britain for images of the towns, villages and streets where their ancestors lived; and, of course, photographs of the churches and chapels where their ancestors were christened, married and buried are an essential part of every genealogy tree and family album.

## FRITH PRODUCTS

All Frith photographs are available Framed or just as Mounted Prints and Posters (size 23 x 16 inches). These may be ordered from the address below. Other products available are - Address Books, Calendars, Jigsaws, Canvas Prints, Postcards and local and prestige books.

## THE INTERNET

Already ninety thousand Frith photographs can be viewed and purchased on the internet through the Frith websites and a myriad of partner sites.

For more detailed information on Frith products, look at this site:
www.francisfrith.com

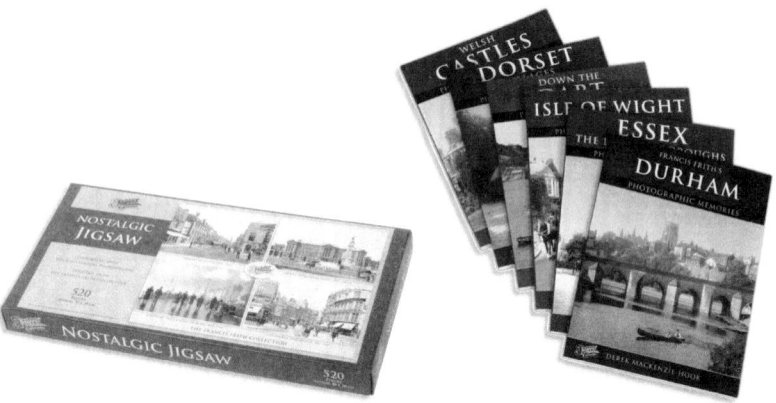

---

**See the complete list of Frith Books at: www.francisfrith.com**
This web site is regularly updated with the latest list of publications from The Francis Frith Collection. If you wish to buy books relating to another part of the country that your local bookshop does not stock, you may purchase on-line.

---

*For further information, trade, or author enquiries please contact us at the address below:*
**The Francis Frith Collection, Unit 6, Oakley Business Park, Wylye Road, Dinton, Wiltshire SP3 5EU.**
Tel: +44 (0)1722 716 376  Fax: +44 (0)1722 716 881  Email: sales@francisfrith.co.uk

---

See Frith products on the internet at www.francisfrith.com

# FREE PRINT OF YOUR CHOICE
## CHOOSE A PHOTOGRAPH FROM THIS BOOK
+ £3.80 POSTAGE

**Mounted Print**
*Overall size 14 x 11 inches (355 x 280mm)*

## TO RECEIVE YOUR FREE PRINT

### Choose any Frith photograph in this book
Simply complete the Voucher opposite and return it with your remittance for £3.50 (to cover postage and handling) and we will print the photograph of your choice in SEPIA (size 11 x 8 inches) and supply it in a cream mount ready to frame (overall size 14 x 11 inches).

### Order additional Mounted Prints
**at HALF PRICE - £12.00 each** (normally £24.00)
If you would like to order more Frith prints from this book, possibly as gifts for friends and family, you can buy them at half price (with no additional postage costs).

### Have your Mounted Prints framed
For an extra £20.00 per print you can have your mounted print(s) framed in an elegant polished wood and gilt moulding, overall size 16 x 13 inches (no additional postage required).

---

**IMPORTANT!**

❶ Please note: aerial photographs and photographs with a reference number starting with a "Z" are not Frith photographs and cannot be supplied under this offer.

❷ Offer valid for delivery to one UK address only.

❸ These special prices are only available if you use this form to order. You must use the ORIGINAL VOUCHER on this page (no copies permitted). We can only despatch to one UK address.

❹ This offer cannot be combined with any other offer.

---

As a customer your name & address will be stored by Frith but not sold or rented to third parties. Your data will be used for the purpose of this promotion only.

*Send completed Voucher form to:*

**The Francis Frith Collection,**
**19 Kingsmead Business Park, Gillingham,**
**Dorset SP8 5FB**

*Voucher* for *FREE* and Reduced Price *Frith Prints*

*Please do not photocopy this voucher. Only the original is valid, so please fill it in, cut it out and return it to us with your order.*

| Picture ref no | Page no | Qty | Mounted @ £12.00 | Framed + £20.00 | Total Cost £ |
|---|---|---|---|---|---|
| | | 1 | Free of charge* | £ | £ |
| | | | £12.00 | £ | £ |
| | | | £12.00 | £ | £ |
| | | | £12.00 | £ | £ |
| | | | £12.00 | £ | £ |
| | | | £12.00 | £ | £ |

*Please allow 28 days for delivery. Offer available to one UK address only*

| | |
|---|---|
| * Post & handling | £3.80 |
| **Total Order Cost** | **£** |

Title of this book . . . . . . . . . . . . . . . . . . . . . . . . . . . . .

I enclose a cheque/postal order for £ . . . . . . . . . . made payable to 'The Francis Frith Collection'

OR please debit my Mastercard / Visa / Maestro card, details below

Card Number:

Issue No (Maestro only):          Valid from (Maestro):

Card Security Number:          Expires:

Signature:

Name  Mr/Mrs/Ms . . . . . . . . . . . . . . . . . . . . . . . . . . .

Address . . . . . . . . . . . . . . . . . . . . . . . . . . . . . . . . . . .

. . . . . . . . . . . . . . . . . . . . . . . . . . . . . . . . . . . . . . . . .

. . . . . . . . . . . . . . . . . . . . . . . . . . . . . . . . . . . . . . . . .

. . . . . . . . . . . . . . . . . . . . Postcode . . . . . . . . . . . . . .

Daytime Tel No . . . . . . . . . . . . . . . . . . . . . . . . . . . . .

Email . . . . . . . . . . . . . . . . . . . . . . . . . . . . . . . . . . . . .

Valid to 31/12/18

Free Print – see overleaf

**Can you help us with information about any of the Frith photographs in this book?**

We are gradually compiling an historical record for each of the photographs in the Frith archive. It is always fascinating to find out the names of the people shown in the pictures, as well as insights into the shops, buildings and other features depicted.

If you recognize anyone in the photographs in this book, or if you have information not already included in the author's caption, do let us know. We would love to hear from you, and will try to publish it in future books or articles.

**An Invitation from The Francis Frith Collection to Share Your Memories**

The 'Share Your Memories' feature of our website allows members of the public to add personal memories relating to the places featured in our photographs, or comment on others already added. Seeing a place from your past can rekindle forgotten or long held memories. Why not visit the website, find photographs of places you know well and add YOUR story for others to read and enjoy? We would love to hear from you!

**www.francisfrith.com/memories**

**Our production team**

Frith books are produced by a small dedicated team at offices near Salisbury. Most have worked with the Frith Collection for many years. All have in common one quality: they have a passion for the Frith Collection.

**Frith Books and Gifts**

We have a wide range of books and gifts available on our website utilising our photographic archive, many of which can be individually personalised.

**www.francisfrith.com**